The Loser Ways

Phenomenal Swear Word To Color

For Stress Releasing

J.N. Moorcroft

Happy Coloring!

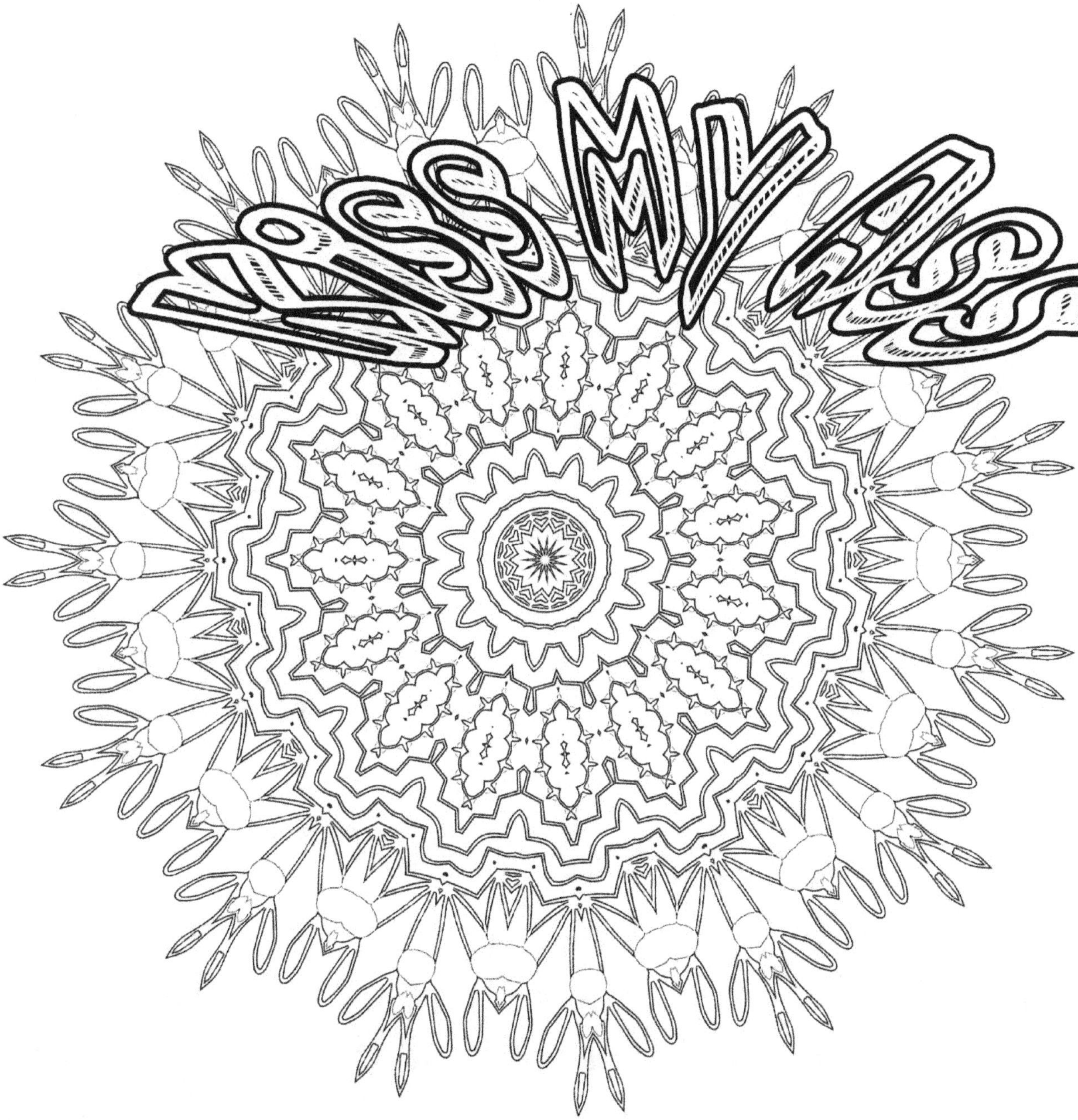
KISS MY ASS

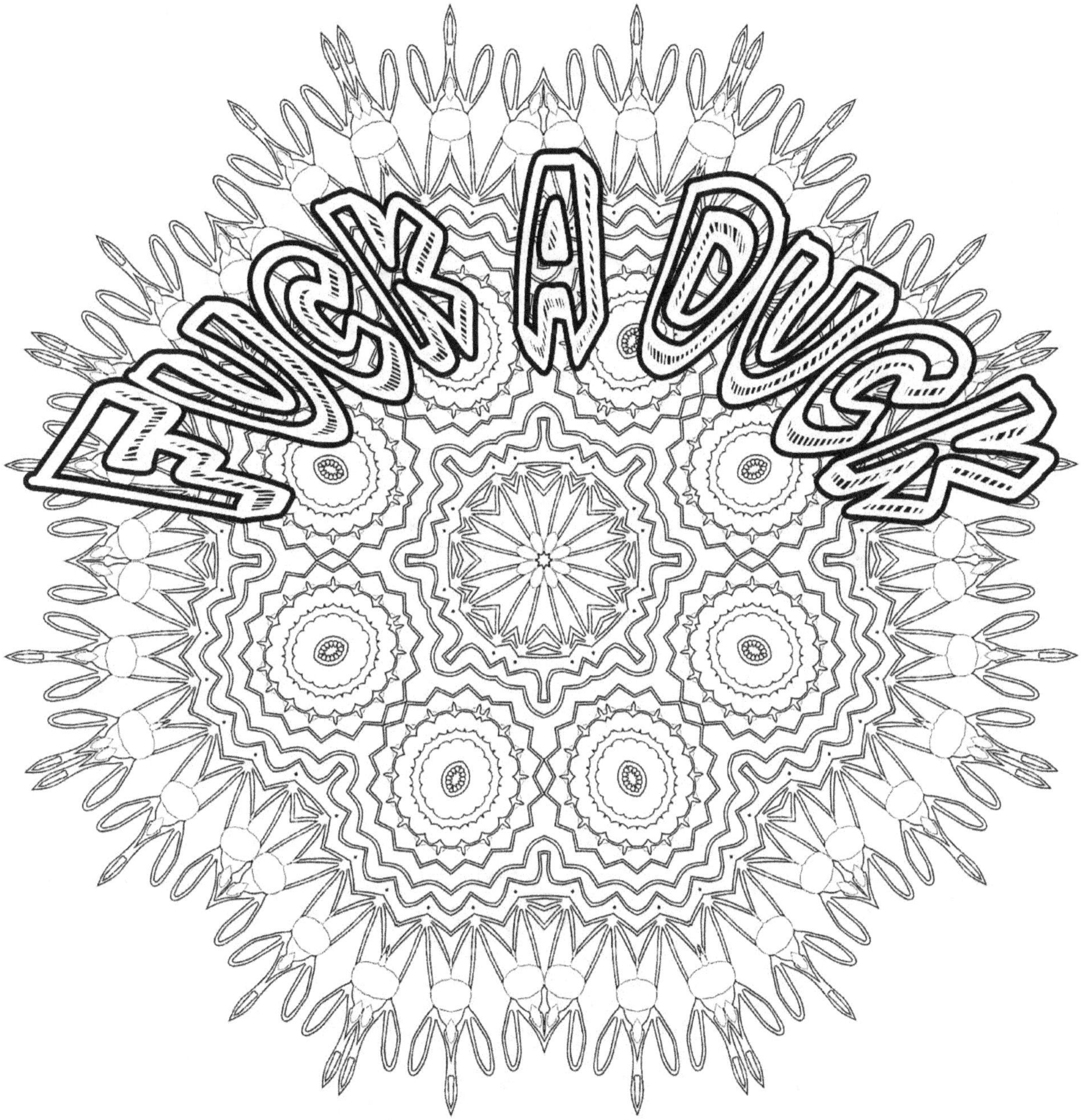
FUCK A DUCK

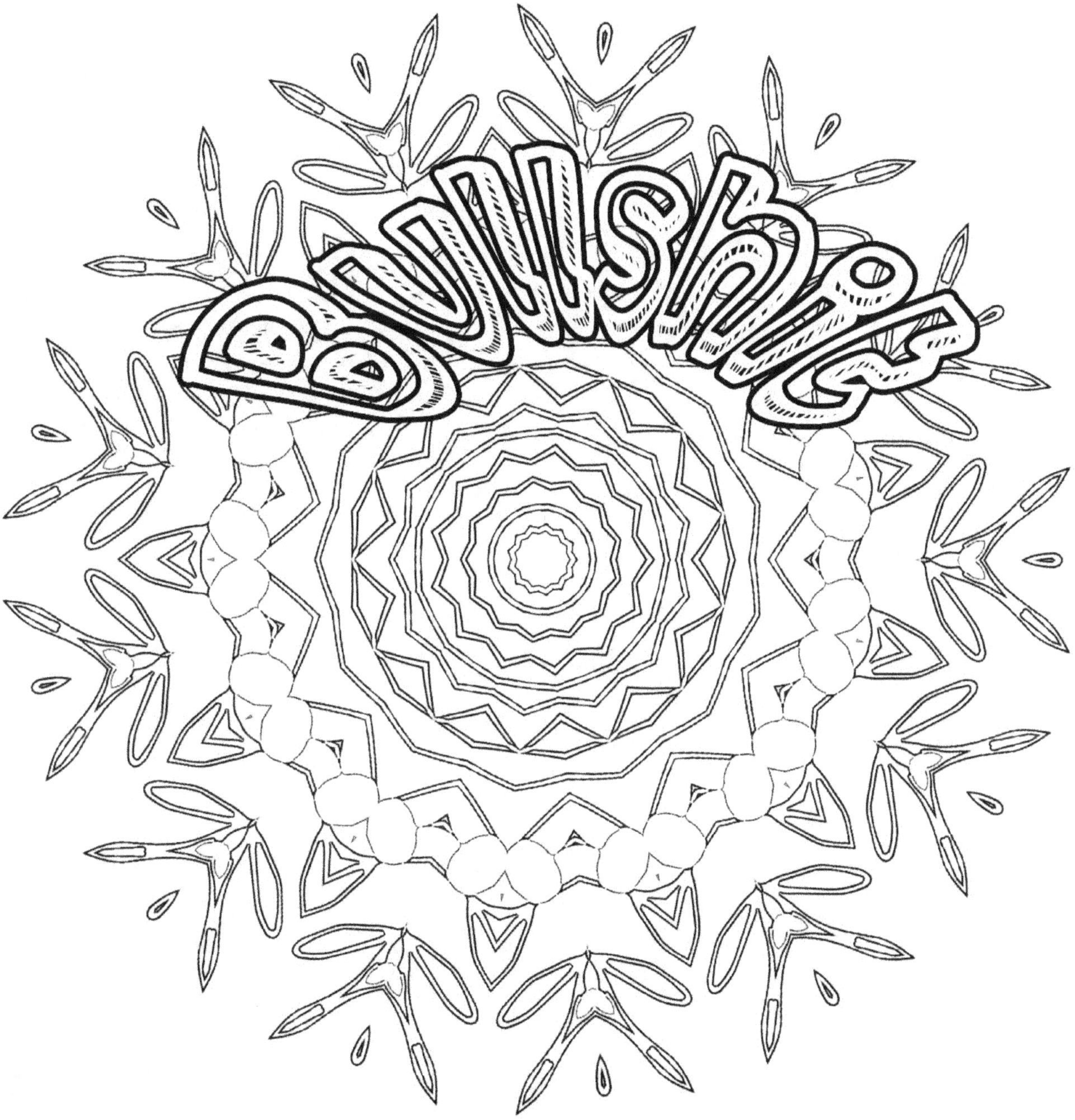
bullshit

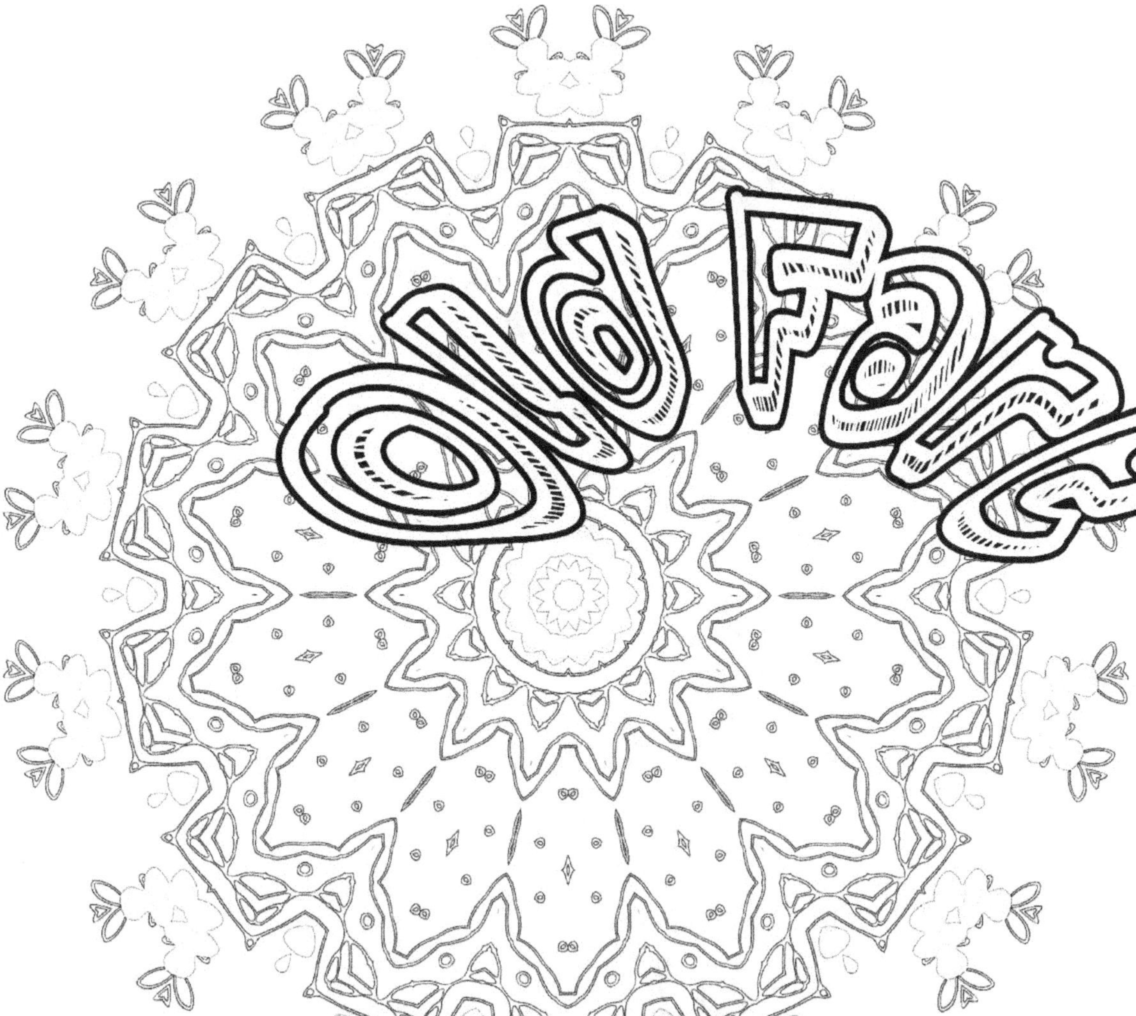
Old Farts

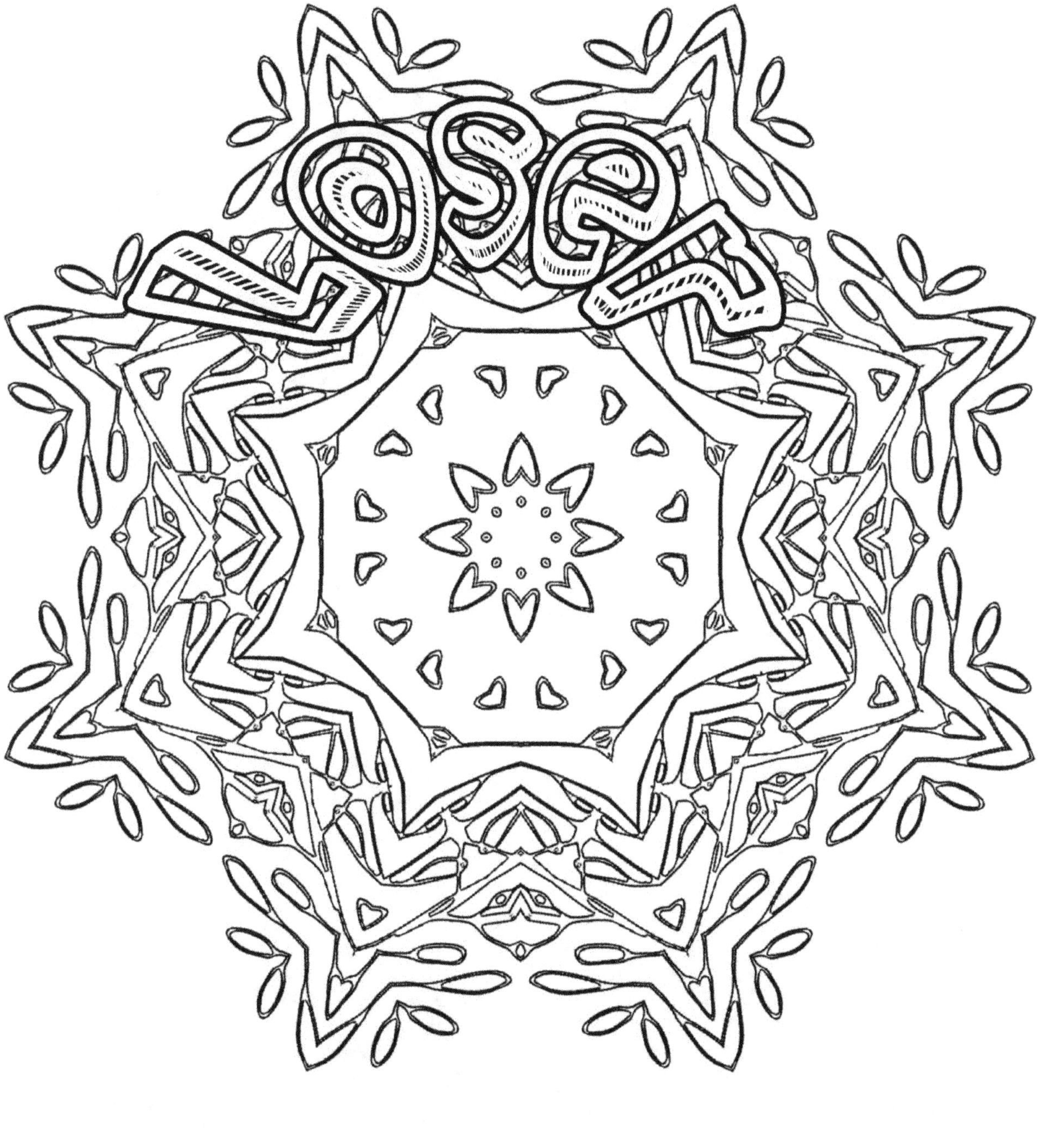
Loser

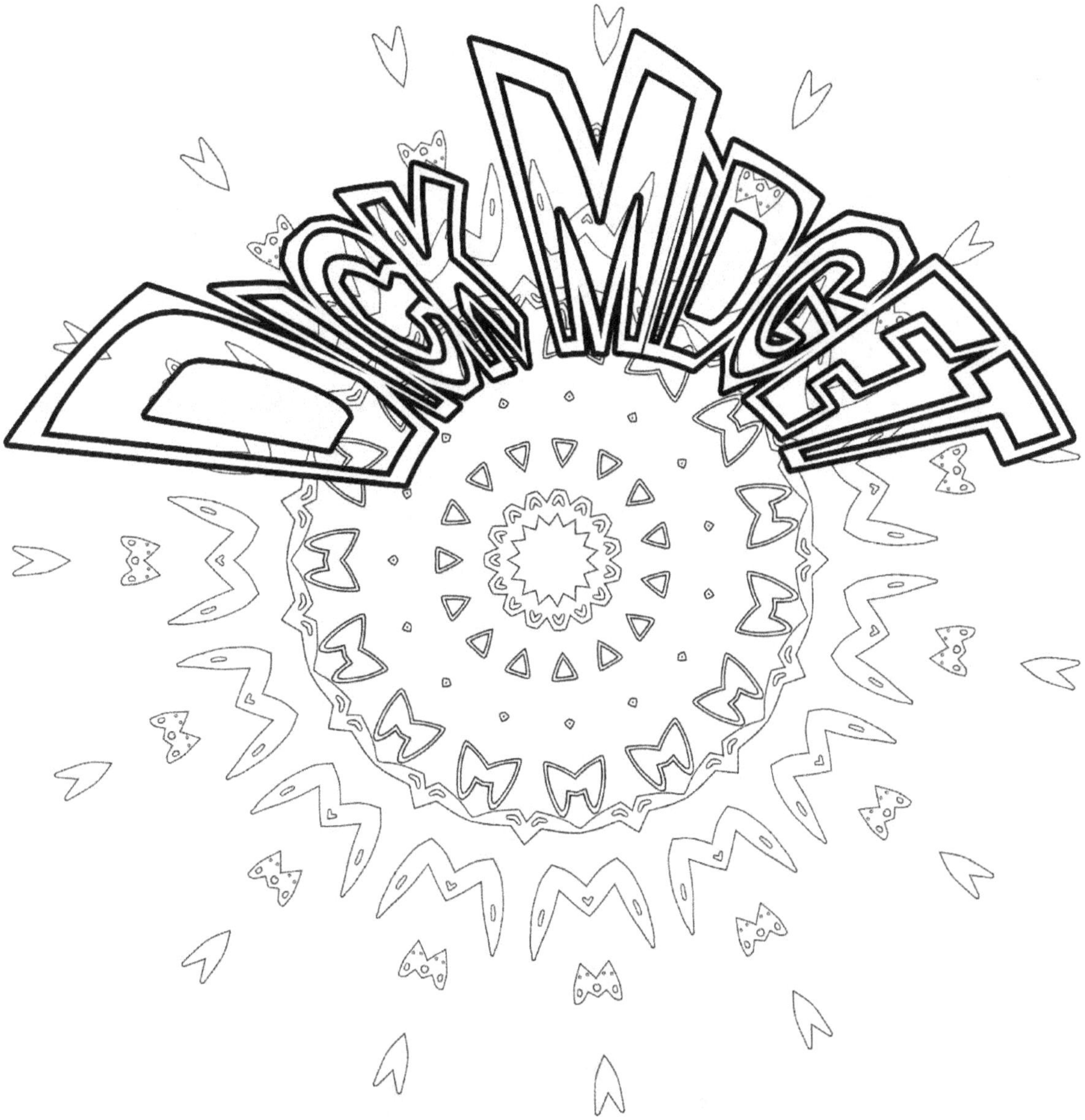

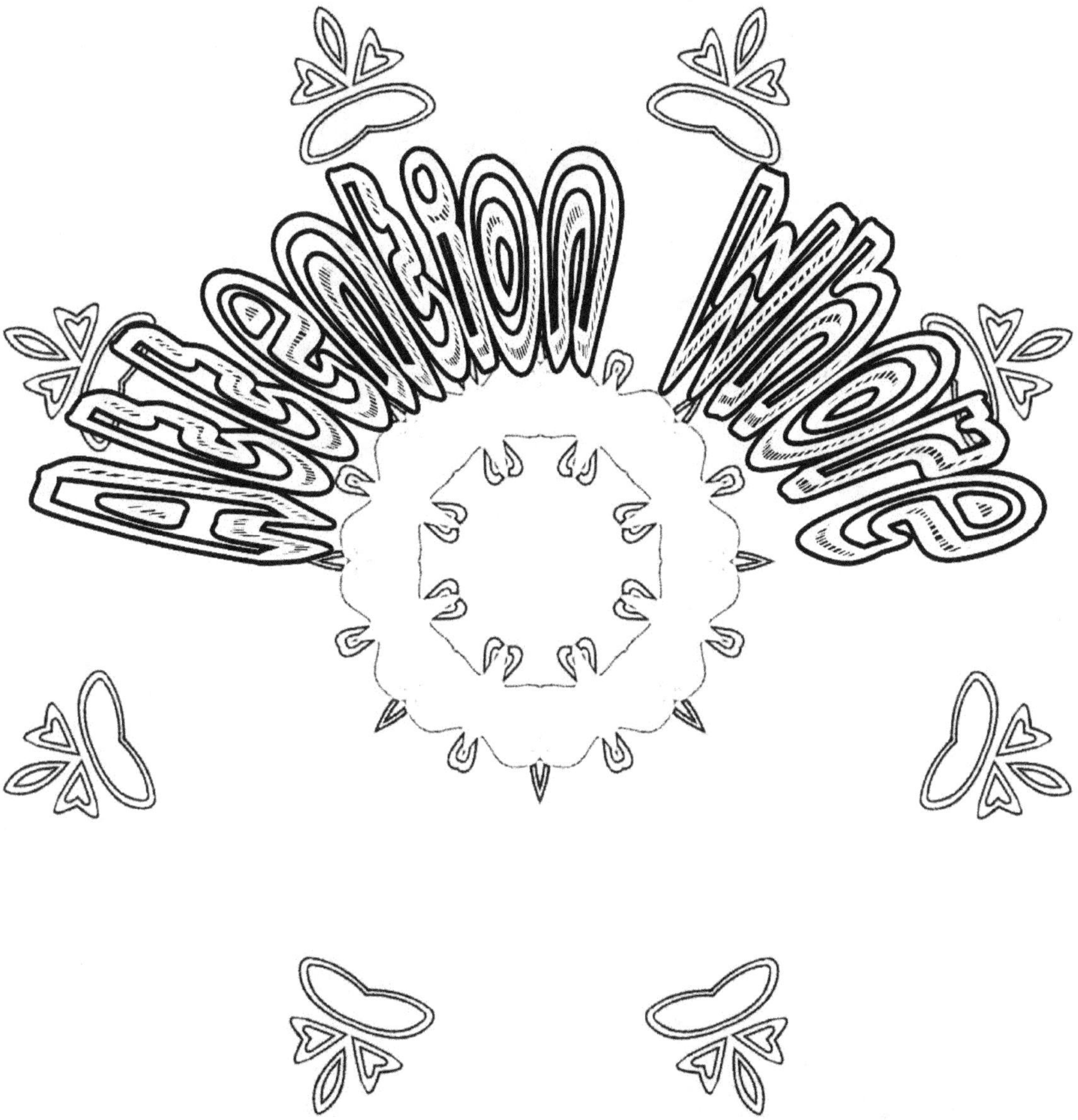
Medication Whore

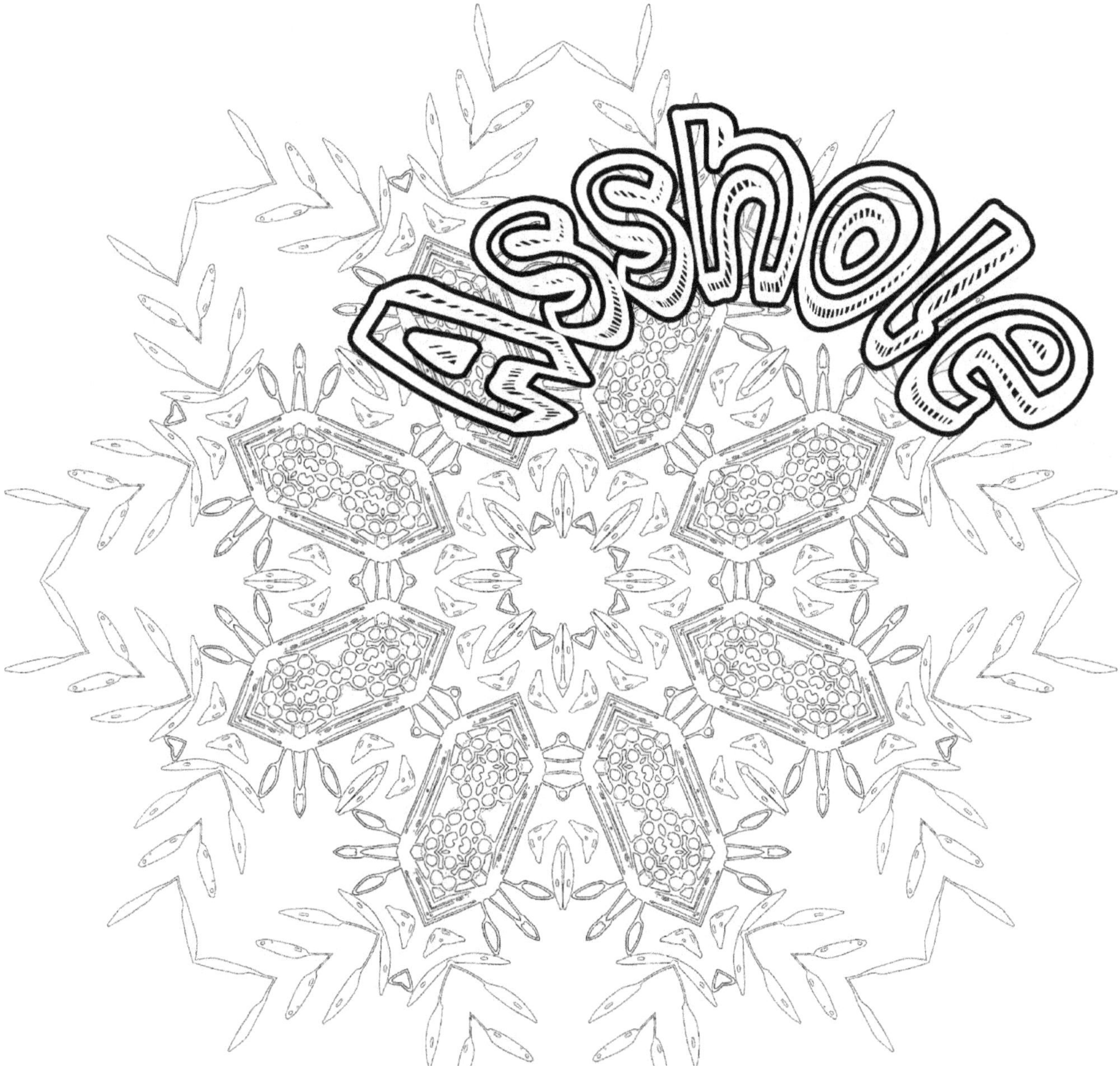
asshole

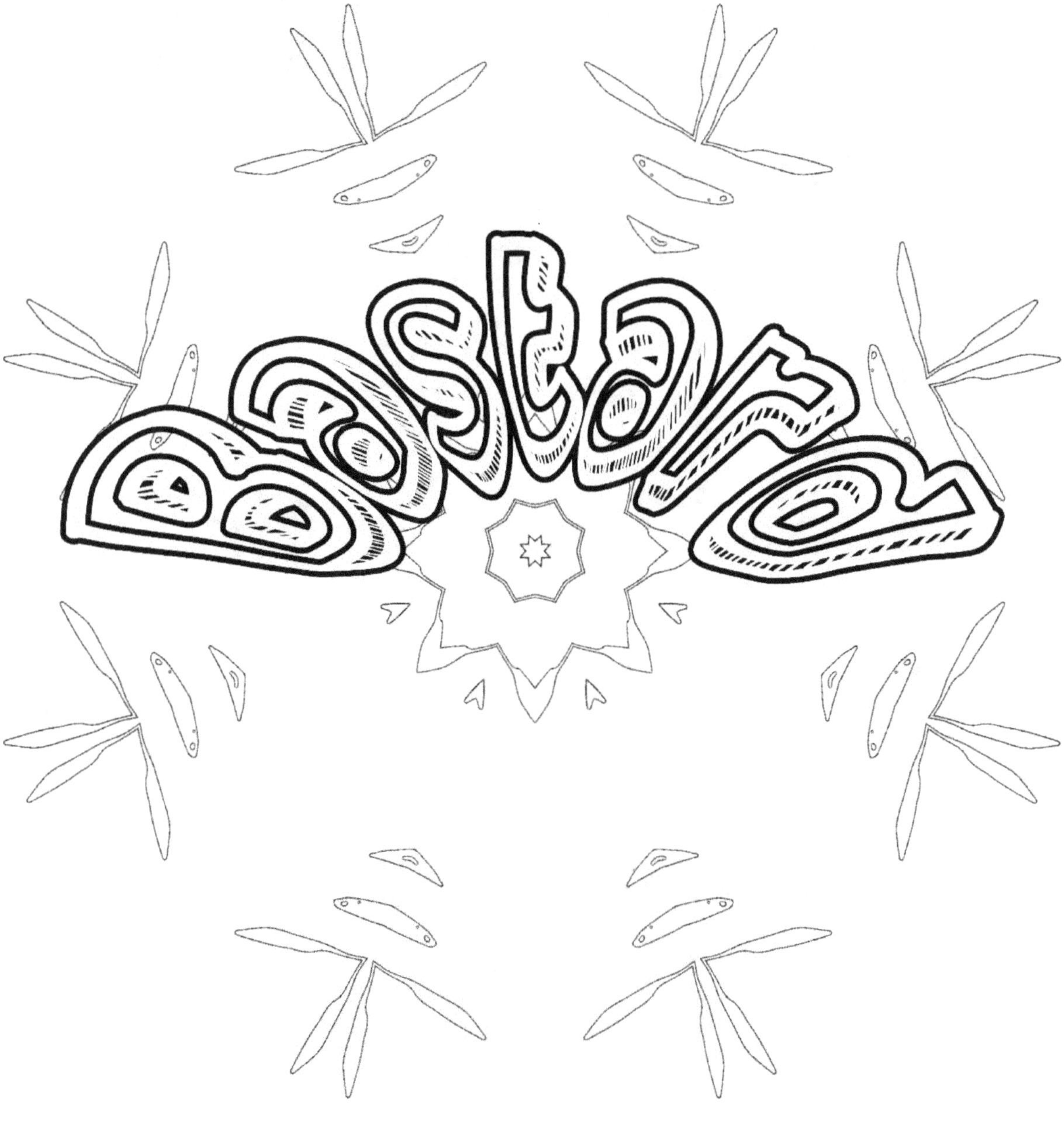
Bastard

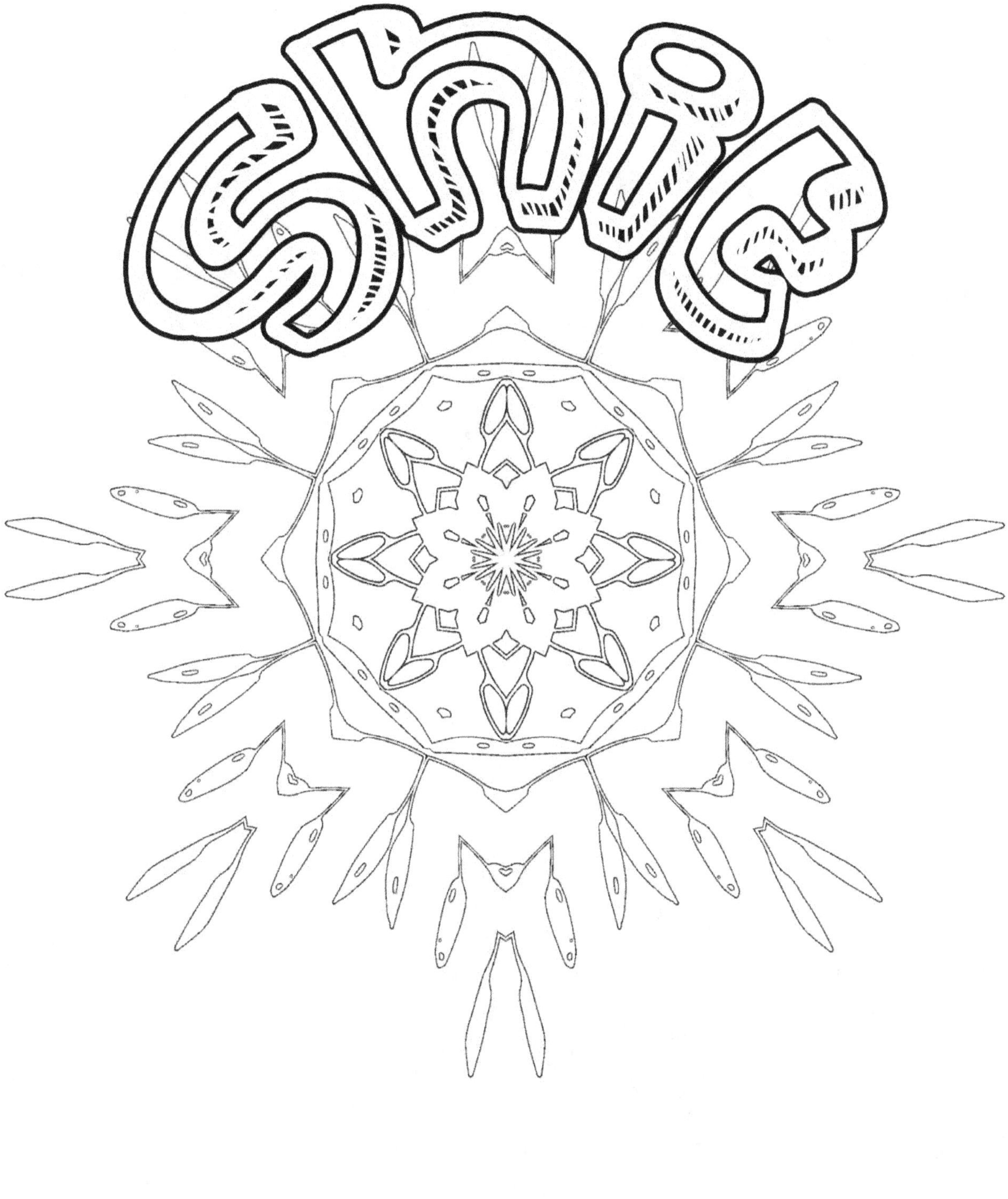
Chic

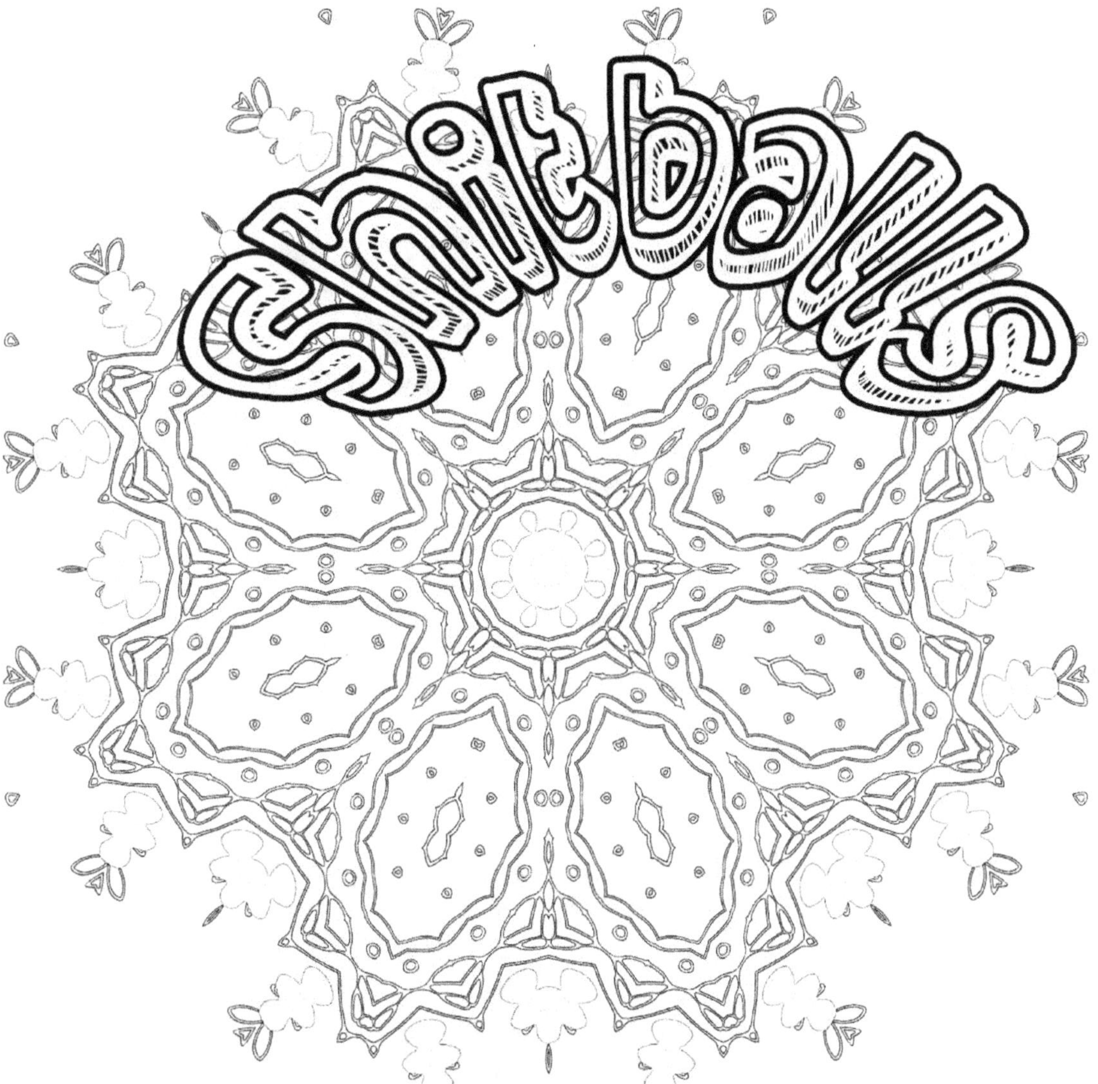
shitballs

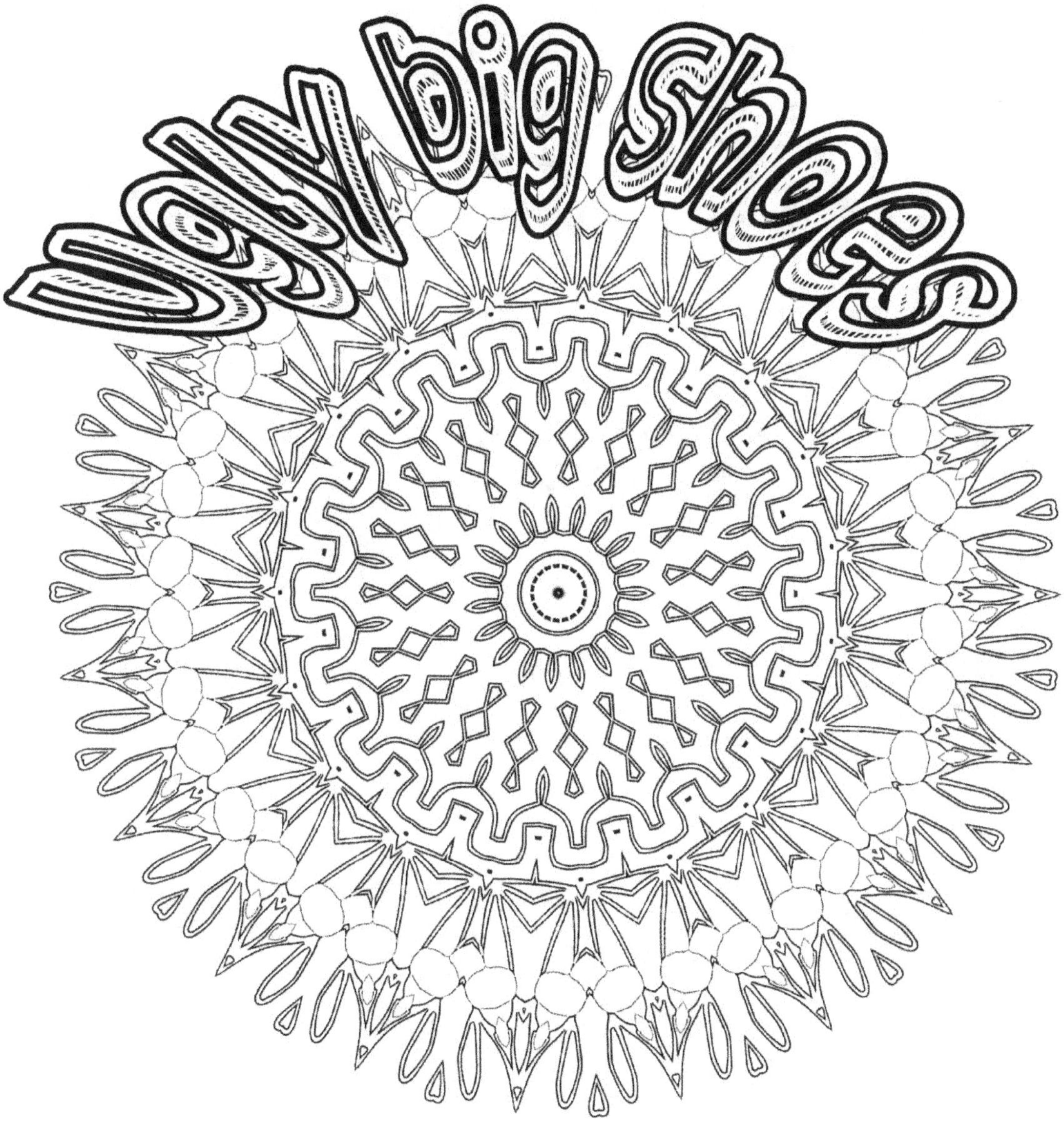
Ugly big Shoes

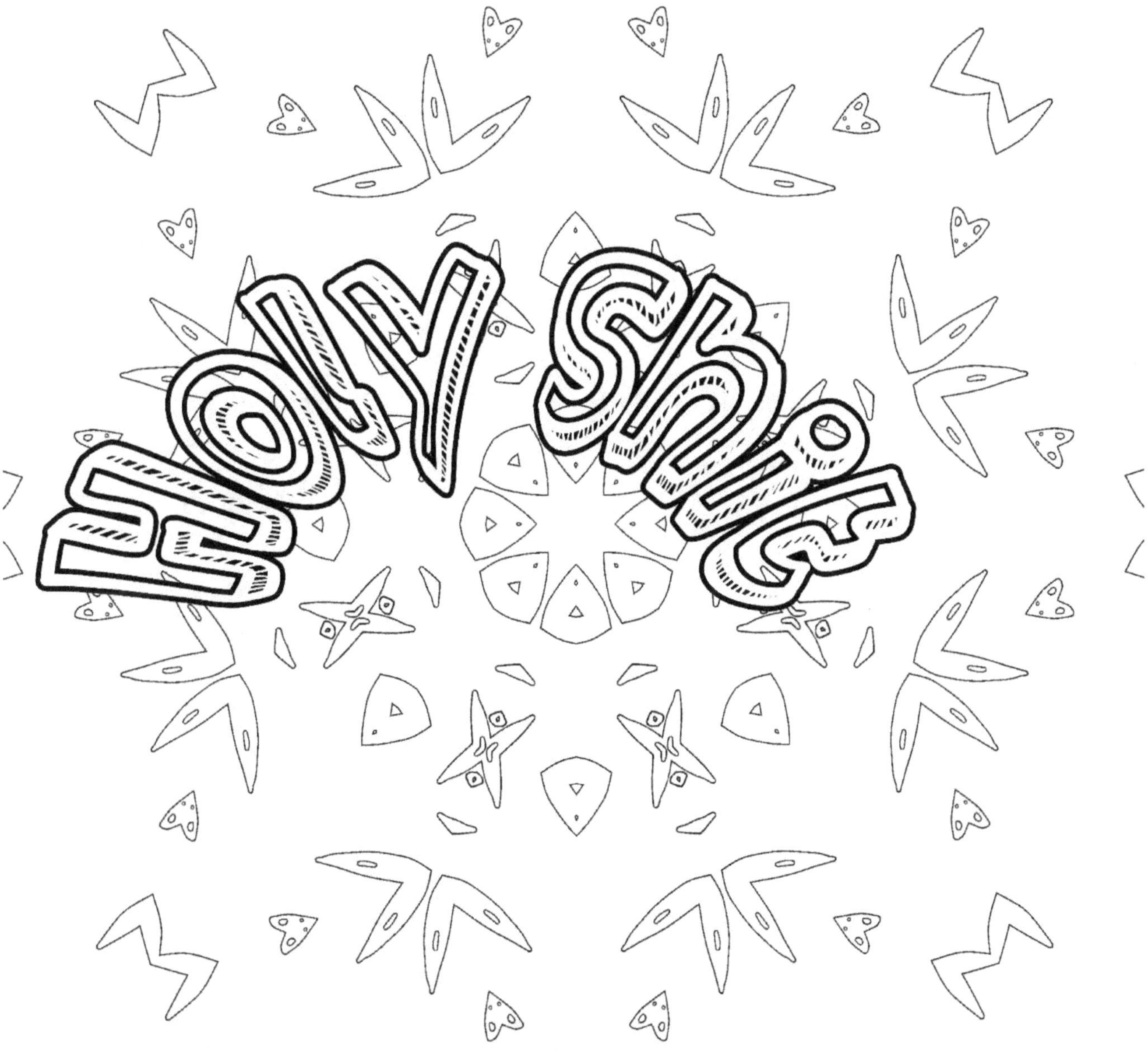
Holy Shit

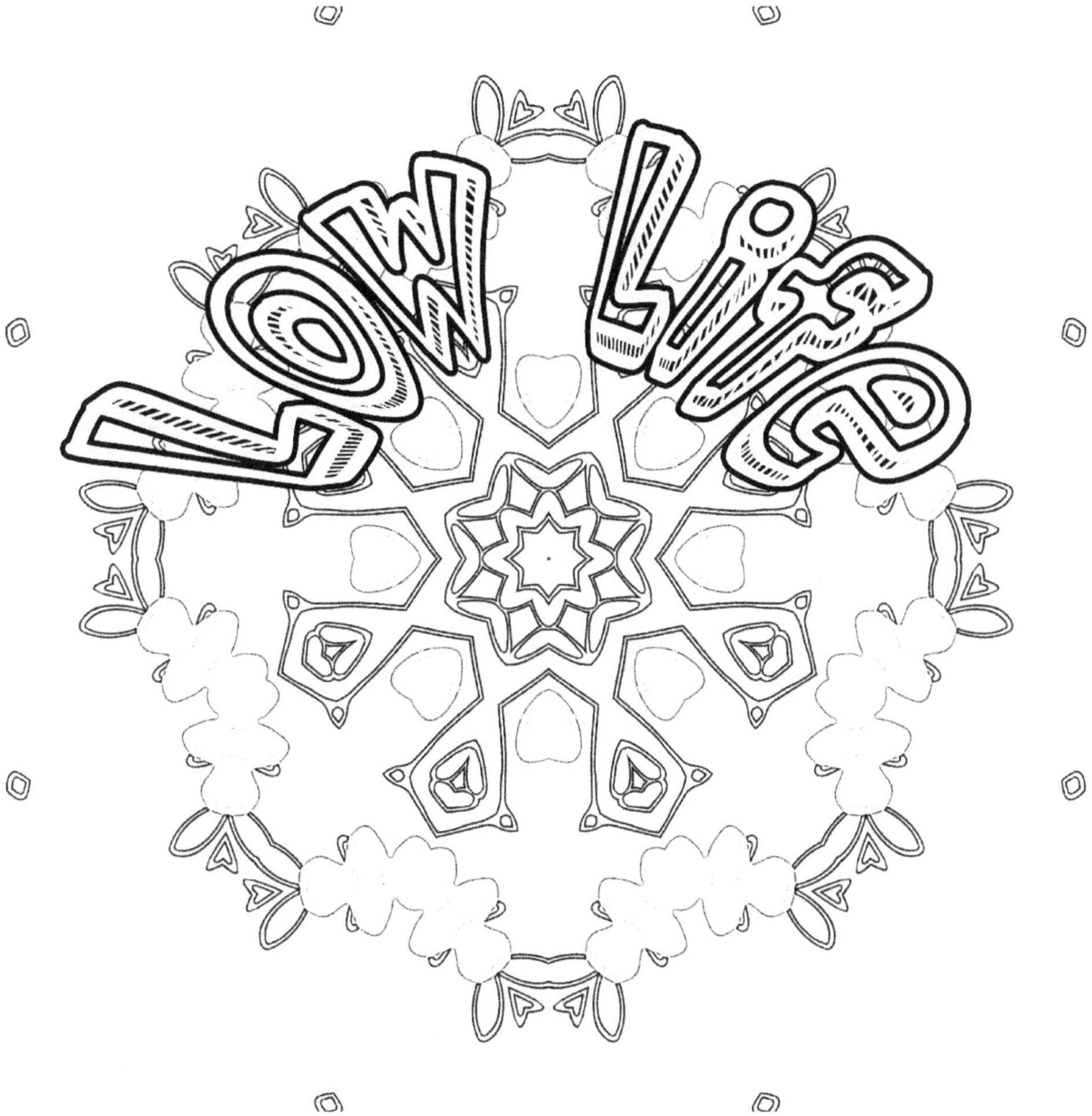
Low Life

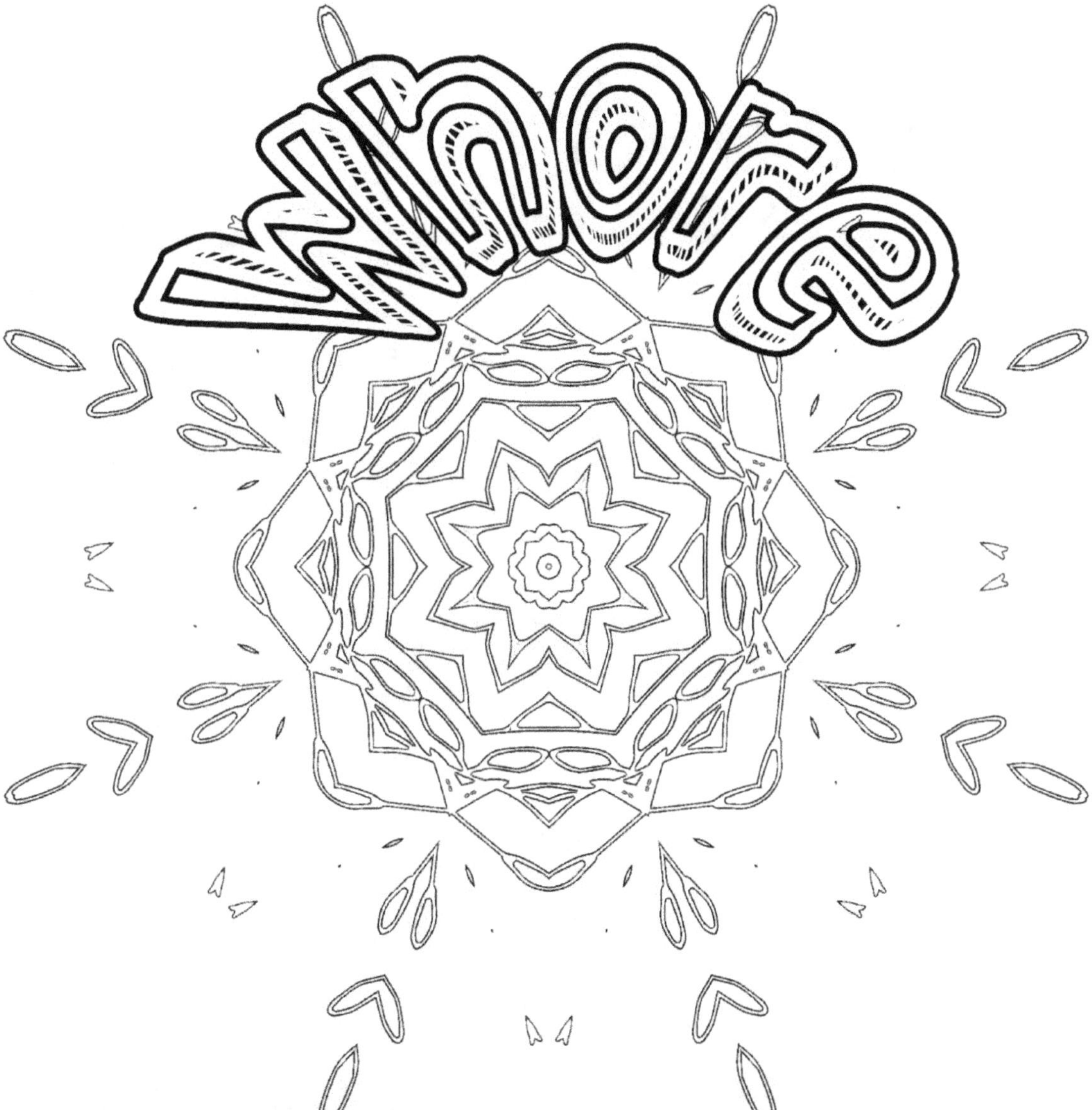
Whore

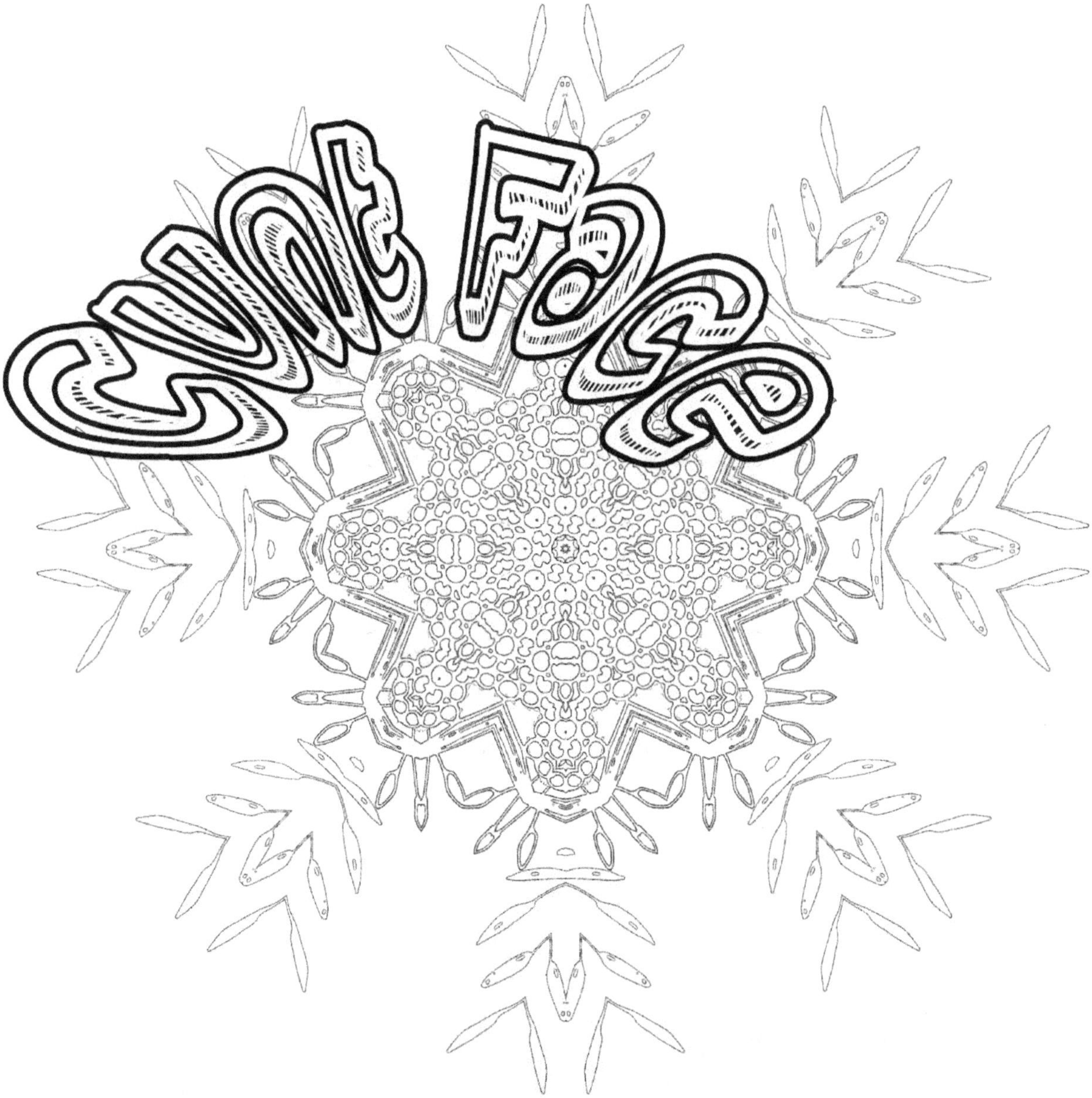
Cunt Face

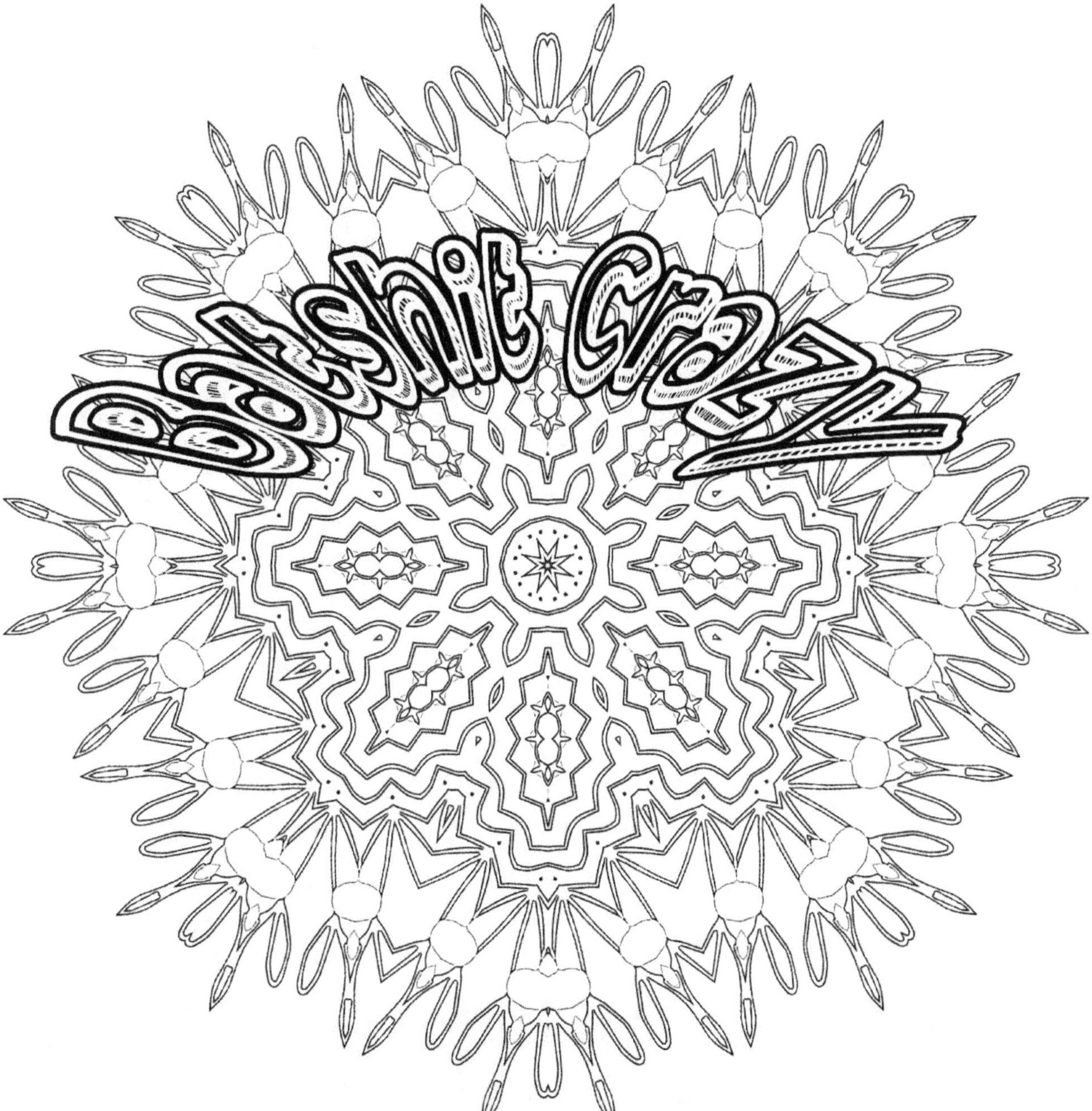
Batshit Crazy

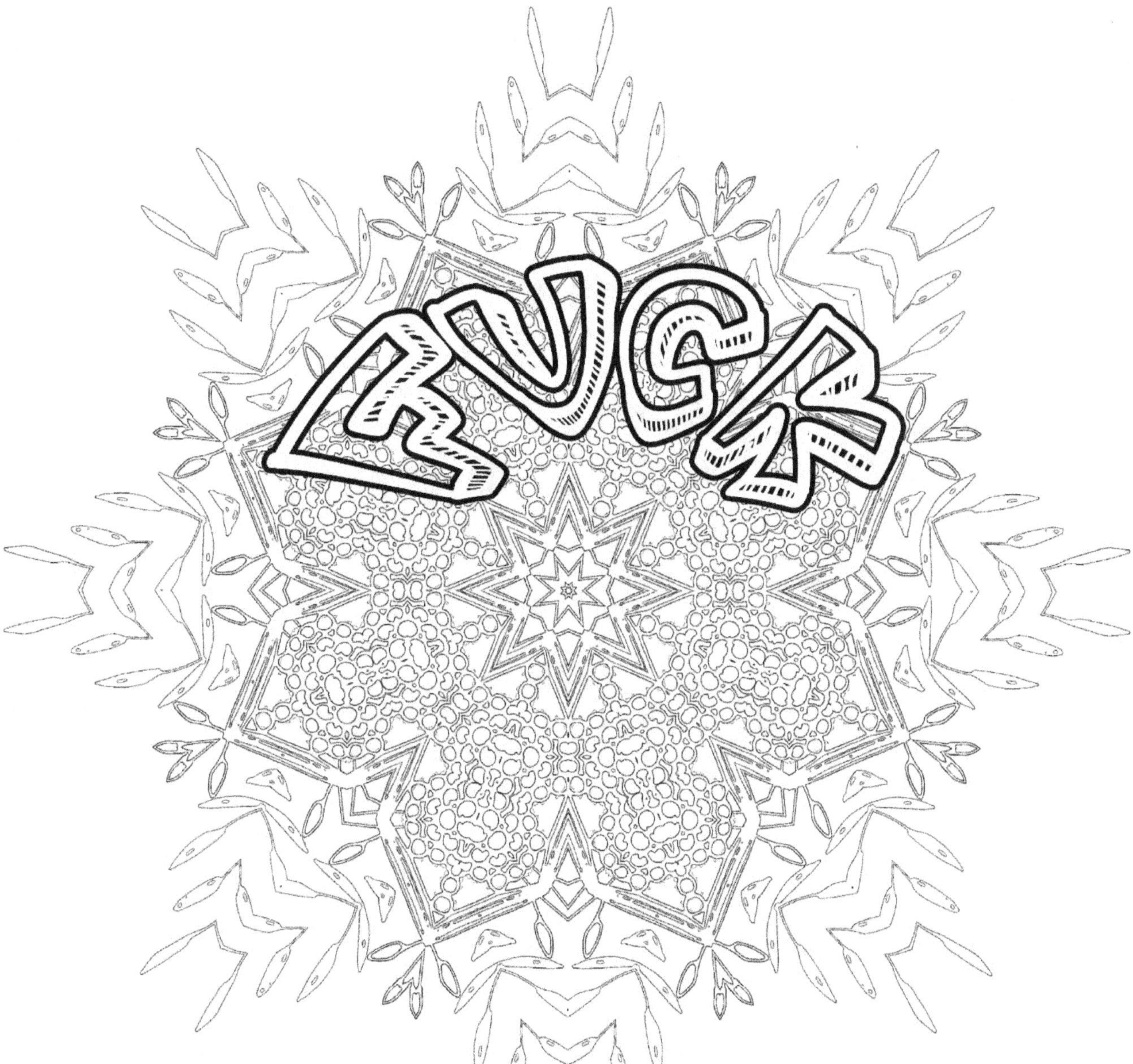
FUCK

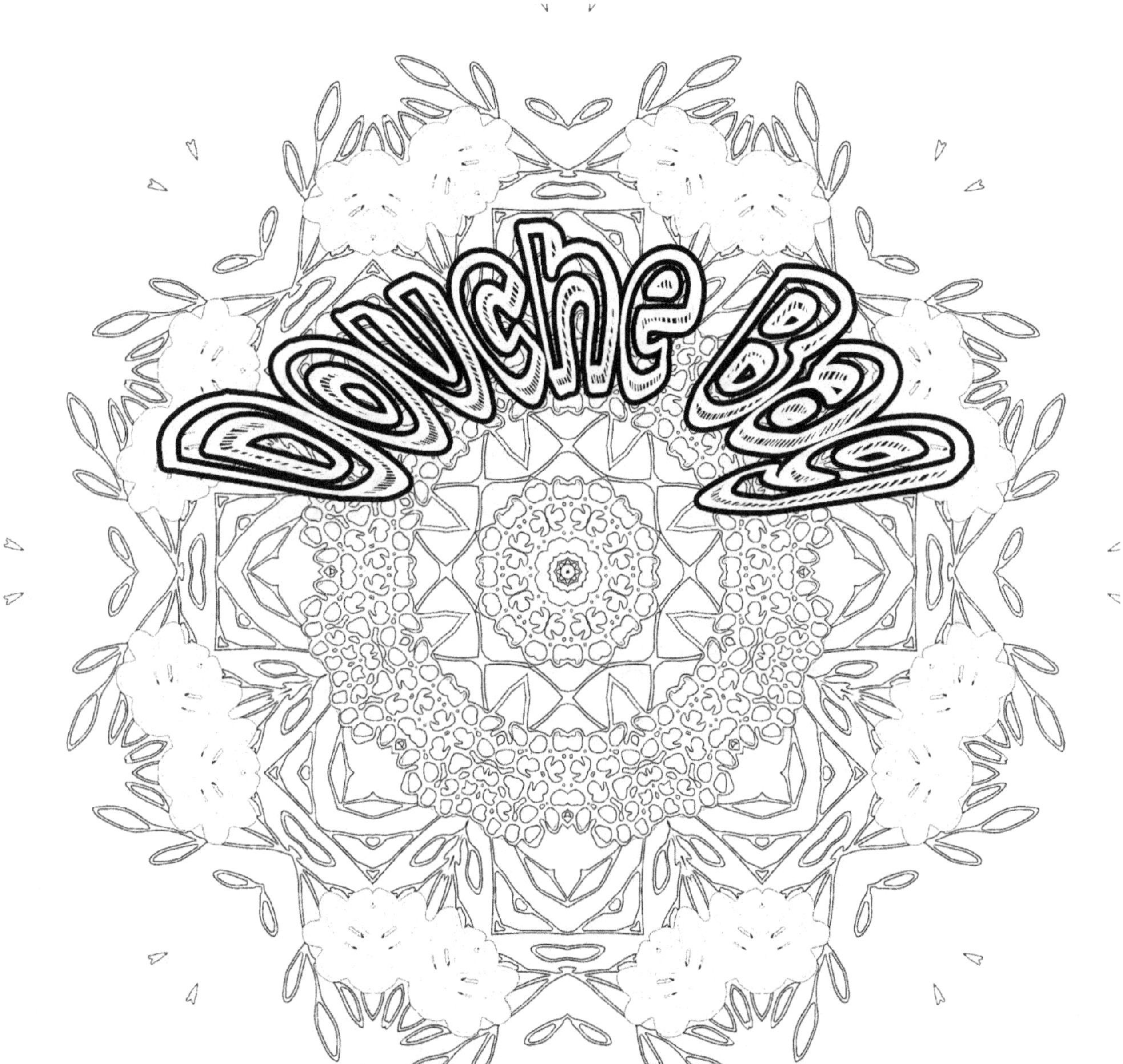
Douche Bag

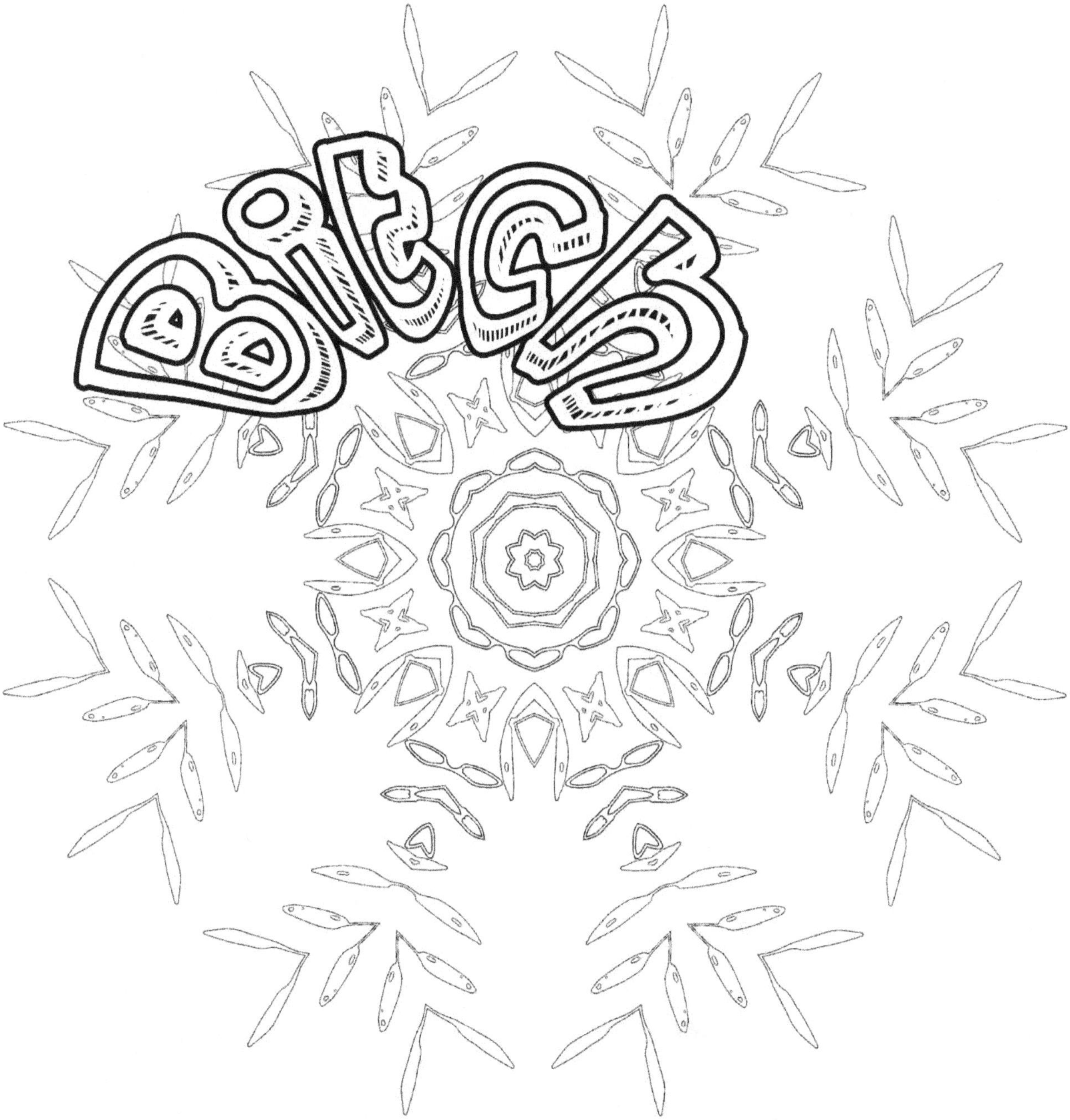
Bitch

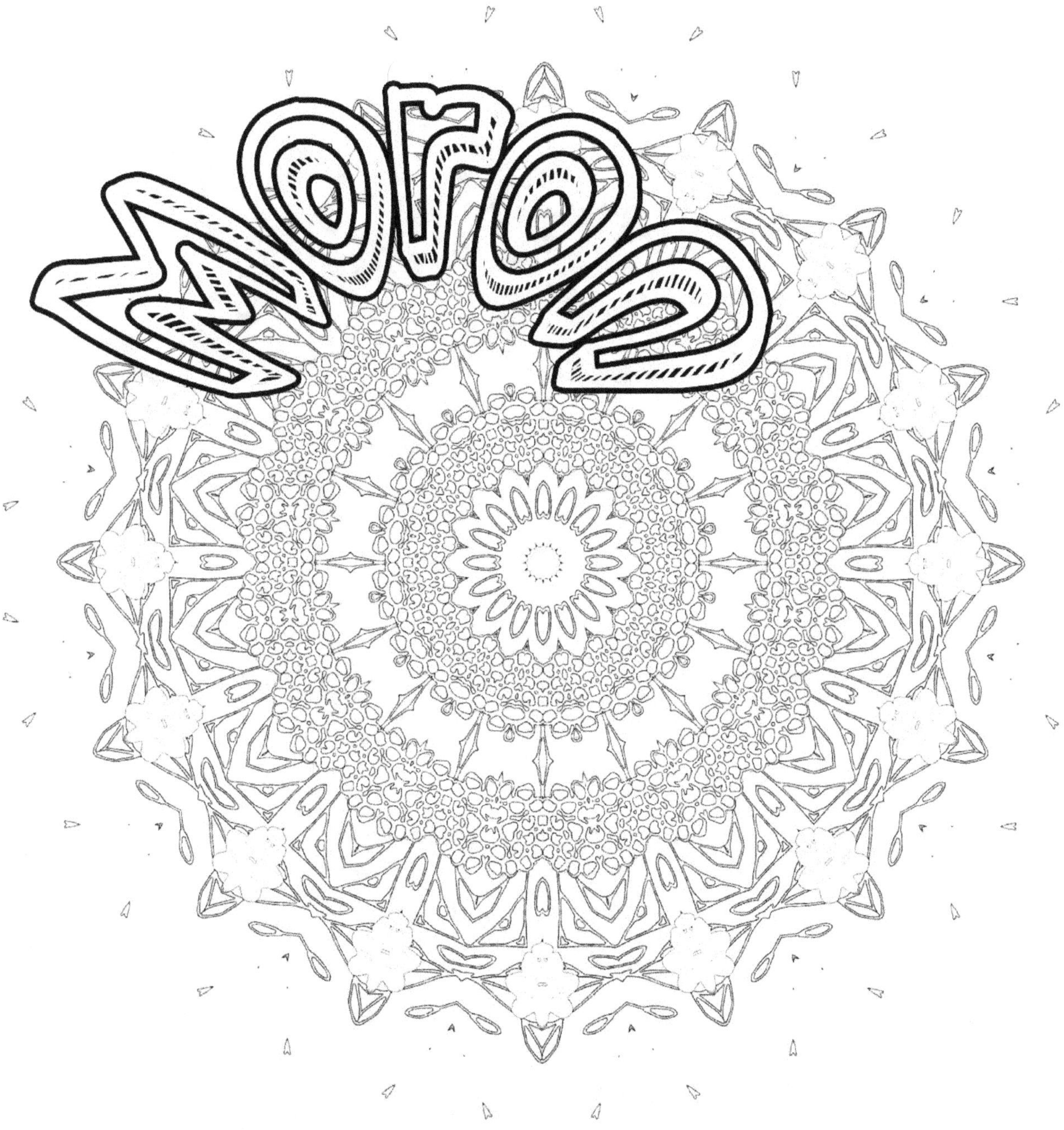
Moron

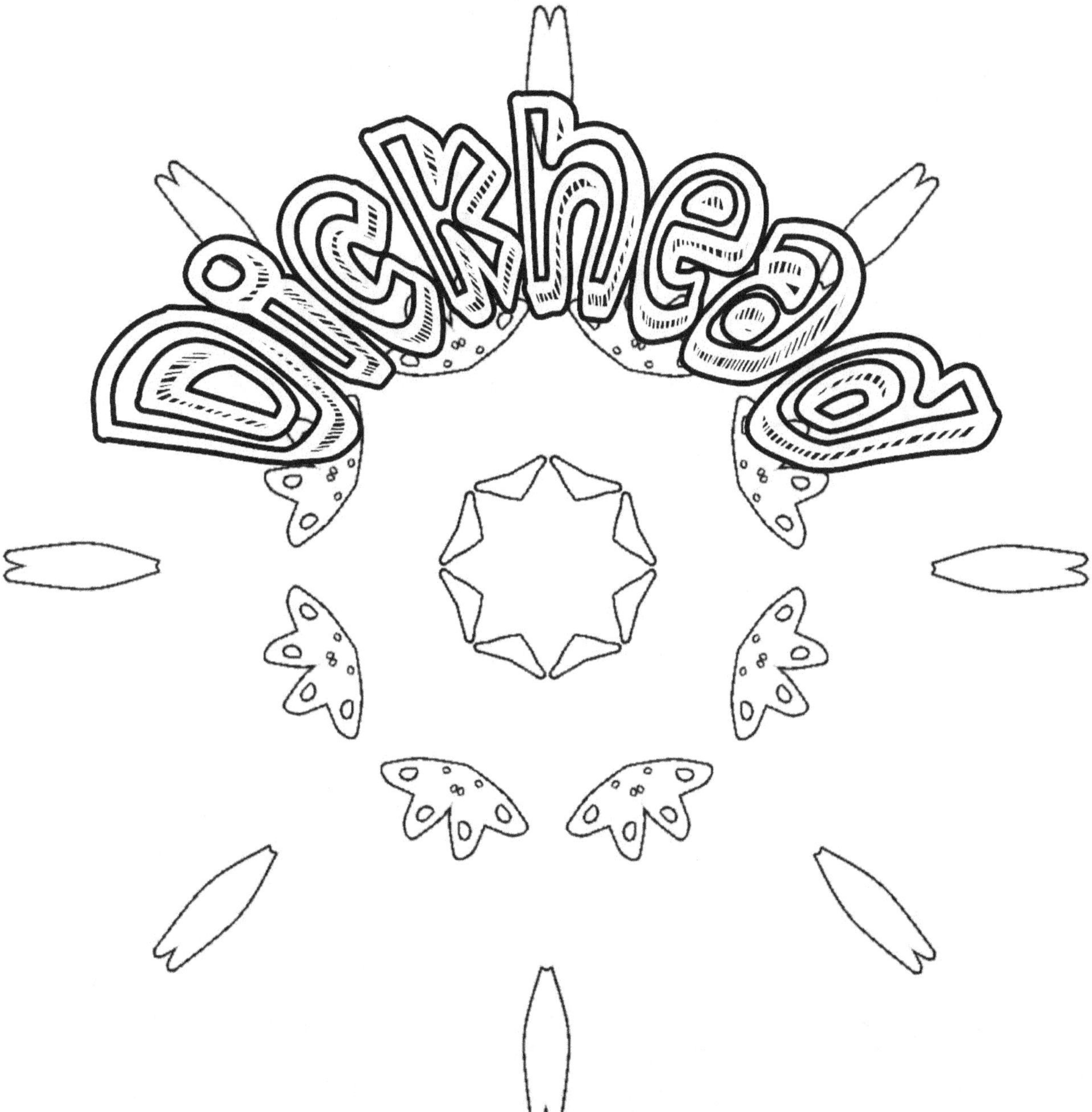
Dickhead

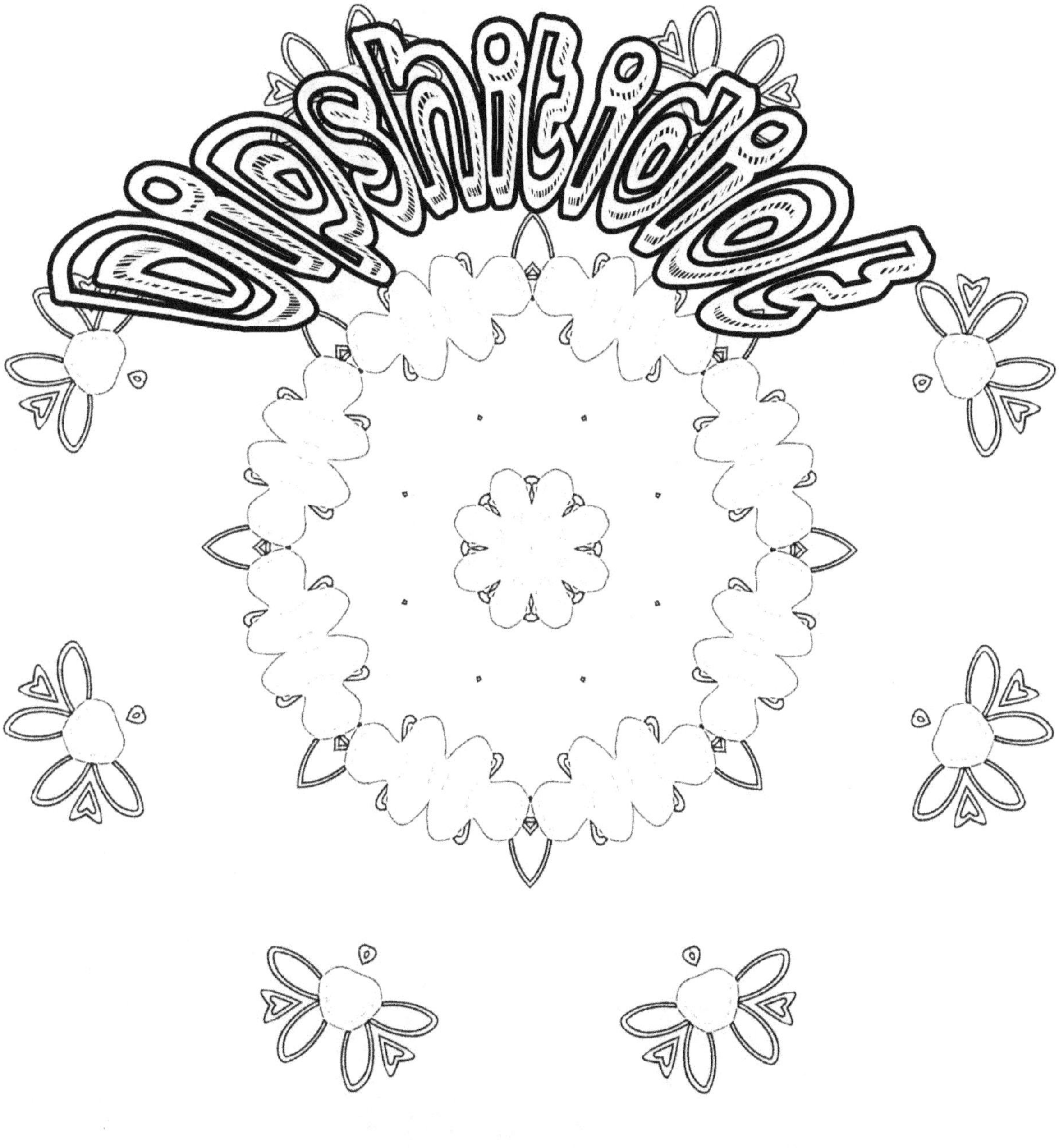

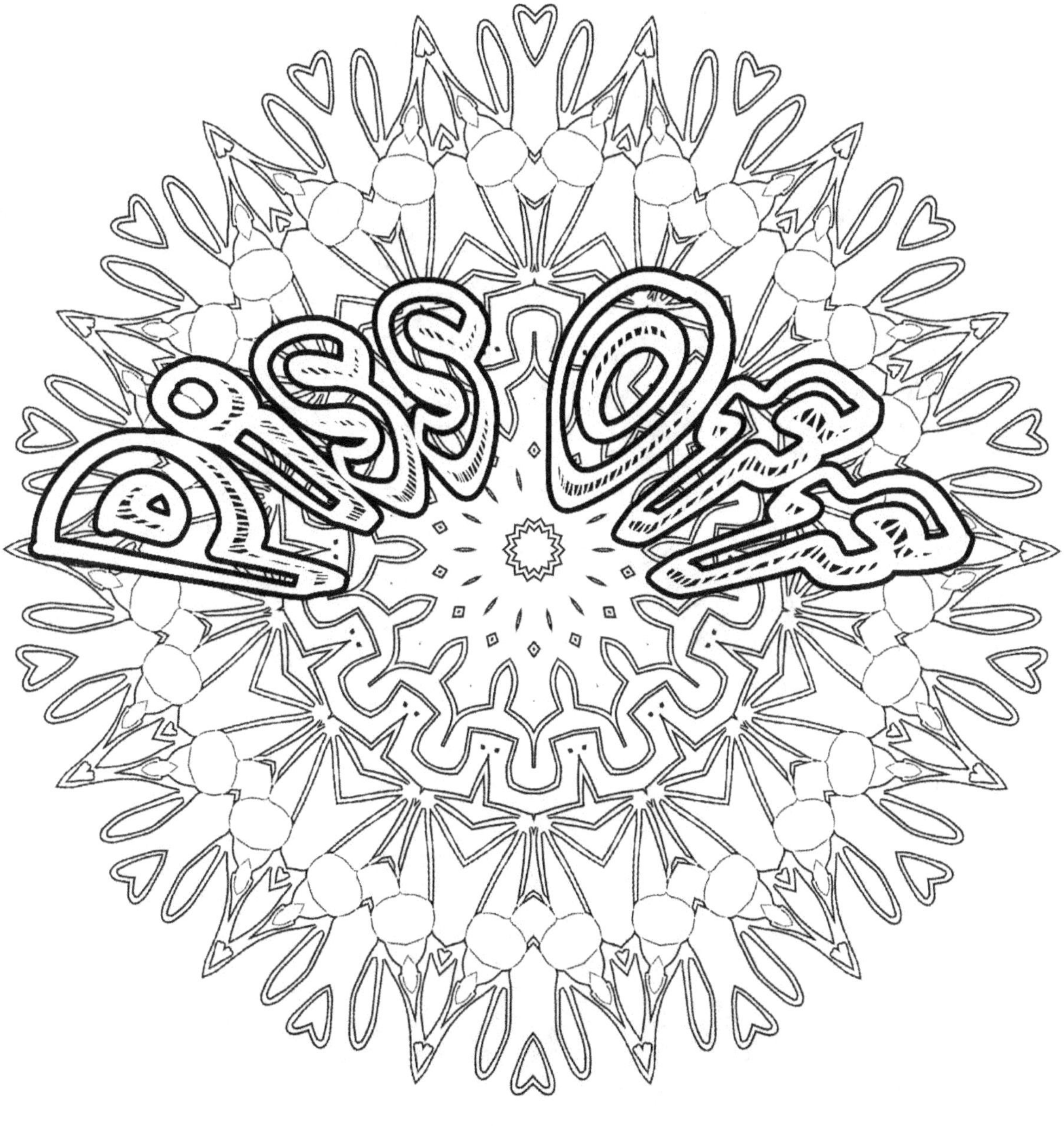
Piss Off

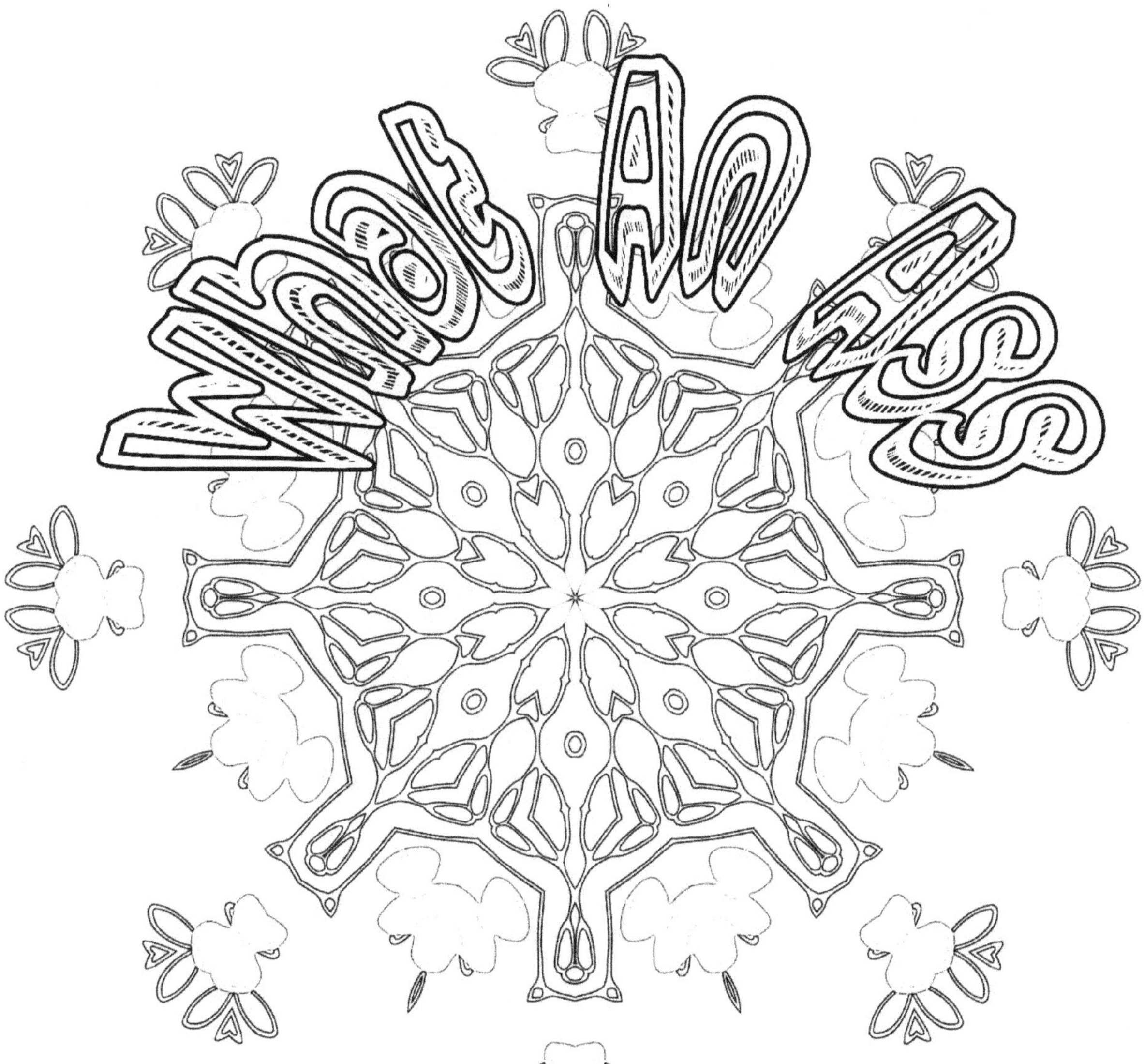
What An Ass

www.ingramcontent.com/pod-product-compliance
Lightning Source LLC
Chambersburg PA
CBHW081750170526
45167CB00009B/3983
9781544181035